This Notebook Belongs To:

Made in the USA
Monee, IL
14 December 2021

85284326R00069